A Guided Guidebook to Yourself

A GUIDED GUIDEBOOK TO YOURSELF

CONNECT WITH YOUR TRUE SELF
TO TRANSFORM YOUR LIFE

RUTH FANKUSHEN, LMFT

ISBN: 979-8-9908574-2-1

COVER DESIGN BY RUTH FANKUSHEN

INTERIOR LAYOUT AND DESIGN BY RUTH FANKUSHEN

PRINTED IN USA

FIRST EDITION: MAY, 2024

RUMAKU

CONTENTS

HELLO

I'm Ruth, an EMDR psychotherapist and artist. For many years, I felt confused, lonely, and anxious. On some level, I knew that I was an okay person, yet I worried all the time. I'm happy to report that through trial and tribulation, and through my training as a transpersonal therapist, I've found some helpful tips, tricks, and tools that have helped me to feel good. I've been able to move forward despite previously-debilitating fears.

Within the pages of this guided journal, you'll learn to quiet your inner critic, recognize your truest self, and strengthen your resilience. The exercises and prompts will illuminate your life in a whole new way. The self-knowledge you gain will guide you to make choices that align with who you really are. And if you're not sure who you are right now, you should have a much better idea by the time you finish this book.

Use this Guided Guidebook on its own or in combination with your personal therapy. If you've never gone to therapy, I believe that this book can serve as a positive pre-therapy experience. Take your time or rush. Doodle and have fun, or be serious. Whatever feels good to you is okay.

Finally, it must be said that although I am a therapist, this book is not in and of itself therapy. If you experience any significantly distressing feelings, please do something else for a while. Consider reaching out to a local therapist. And if you're in crisis, call or text 988, or go to a local emergency room.

You deserve to feel good.

Warmly, Ruth Fankushen, LMFT aka Ru Fanku
California, May 2024

TAMING STRESS

Knowing how to regulate your feelings can be like carrying a flashlight, map, and first aid kit. When you learn to identify your triggers and reactions, you're much more prepared to handle them. As a result, you gain more self-control and confidence and begin to plan how you want to behave and feel.

You may have suffered trauma, and it might be difficult to believe that you can heal. That makes sense. I want to let you know that in my work as an EMDR trauma therapist, I have witnessed clients discover peace and joy within themselves, despite having lived through extremely difficult experiences. It's an honor to be with individuals as they locate and explore their inner guiding lights, their own inner supports.

Before diving deep into your interior landscapes, let's prepare. This next section includes my favorite coping skills. Learning how to tame stress naturally increases safety.

When people begin to feel safer and more in control of their daily emotional experiences, they can more easily gain perspective and access the good stuff that life has to offer.

MY USUAL STRESS REACTIONS

Without judging yourself, write down some ways that you sometimes react to stressful situations. (Ex: "I withdraw when I feel my value is being questioned." or "I start to be aggressive when people don't offer to help me, especially since I'm always helping them.")

HOW I CURRENTLY DEACTIVATE STRESS

Write about the things you do that help you feel less stressed. Some methods may be more effective than others.

CREATING A CONTAINER

In therapy, the idea of emotional containment is important. Containers help humans keep it all together. Therapy sessions are containers. This book is a container. Our schools and job descriptions are containers. Our homes can be containers. Containers are defined spaces that can help to guide us and manage our thoughts and emotions by holding them.

Imagine a special container for holding your upsetting thoughts, images, and/or feelings. You might picture a safe, a vault, bottle with a top, or a lock box, or locker. You should be the only one who knows the combination or who has the key.

You can access this container whenever you need to store troubling material. Or you can open it when you want to think about or process on these stored thoughts or feelings.

Or you can leave the material inside the container. You don't have to deal with it. These thoughts and feelings are yours. They're safe in your container.

THE MENTAL CONTAINER

Describe what your container looks like. Is it a safe, a vault, a lock box, or something else?

Where does your container exist in your imagination? Is it on top of a mountain or under the sea? Is it in your therapist's office or guarded by dragons?

WINDOW OF TOLERANCE

When we're within the Window of Tolerance (a Dan Siegel, MD term), we're in the emotional state where we feel like we can manage and cope with our emotions, and where we're able to think and feel at the same time. A goal in therapy is often to expand this window so that clients can function better and ride out upsetting, surprising, or confusing situations more easily.

Sometimes the impact of upsetting memories or situations can hijack our coping capacities. All of a sudden, we can get hypo-aroused (sleepy, spaced out, have a hard time talking, etc.) or we can feel hyper-aroused (frozen, anxious, scared, tense) or we may engage in fawning behavior to stay safe (ex: trying to please others by pushing our own needs aside.)

Often we're not aware that our trauma responses have been activated. But bodies remember past events. Even small things (like the air temperature, or someone's gesture, tone of voice, perfume, or the way they cook their eggs) can confuse our systems. These things may remind us (and our bodies) about a past traumatic situation.

Recognizing when we're actually safe in the moment (when that's the case) is an important step towards tolerating feelings in a more regulated and functional way. Grounding techniques can help us get into and stay within the window of tolerance.

7

THE WINDOW OF TOLERANCE AND ME

Can you briefly identify a time or two when you've been outside of the Window of Tolerance? Identify what that looked like for you. Were you shut down, avoidant, frozen, panicked, or did you fawn (exhibit behavior to please someone else in order to cope)?

I AND THE TREE ARE THE SAME

This is a good exercise to do when you want to feel calm and grounded and feel like a tree. You could record the following script onto your phone, or have a trusted person read it for you. Then find a quiet spot to sit or stand without interruptions. Close your eyes or keep them open, and play back the recording. I also like the idea of having a friend read the script aloud to you in real time.

The Script:

"Breathe deeply and visualize a sturdy, majestic tree as you breathe. Notice the season and feel the air. What does it feel like? Embody the essence of the tree you've chosen. Envision your body as the tree, with roots extending into the ground from your feet. Imagine your arms as branches, your body as the trunk, and your legs and feet as the roots reaching deep, deep, deep into the Earth.

Whether you're seated or standing, acknowledge the connection between your feet and the ground. Feel the stability and support from the trunk and roots.

Shift your focus to your breath. Inhale strength from the sky through your branches and exhale stress out through the roots into the Earth beneath your feet. Take a moment to feel rooted and connected to the Earth."

IF I WAS A TREE

If you were a tree, what kind of tree would you be? Where would you be planted? Who would take care of you?

SOME WAYS TO FEEL BETTER

Be curious about your emotions without judging yourself.

Notice the presence of any strong emotions. Say to yourself, "There's that familiar feeling again," or "Oh yeah, I recognize this feeling."

Describe your emotional experience as, "I feel (sad)" rather than, "I am (a sad person)." This little edit creates some distance and inner space. Changing the way we talk about our problems can stop us from putting ourselves down and over-identifying with limiting conditions. Remember that you are not your emotion.

Try not to act impulsively when you're feeling bad. People hardly ever make great decisions when they're coming from a place of worry. (Ask me later.)

Notice other feelings you are experiencing at the same time as your dominant emotion. For instance, you may be freaking out, but are you also hungry? Are you also curious about what you'll wear to the party next week? Difficulties can feel smaller when they're set alongside other feelings or thoughts.

Experience your emotion like a wave, coming in and going out. Ride the wave.

HOW TO GET GROUNDED

If you notice yourself panicking, try saying to yourself:

- *This feeling will go away.*
- *A panic attack can't harm me*
- *I am breathing*
- *I'm beginning to feel more relaxed*
- *I'll feel better soon*
- *I've felt differently before*
- *People all over the world feel the same way as I do, right at this moment*
- *Notice where you're sitting. Feel your body in the chair. Feel the chair. Say to yourself: "All that is actually happening in this moment is that I'm sitting in this chair."*

This feeling is temporary

HOW TO GET GROUNDED

This is a good exercise to do if you're ever feeling dissociated, floaty, or like you're not really real or that things around you aren't real. It can be confusing and disconcerting when this happens. Please reach out to a medical professional if these types of feelings persist or cause you distress. Passing instances of dissociation are common.

Identify:
- *5 things you see*
- *4 things you feel*
- *3 things you hear*
- *2 things you smell*
- *1 thing you taste*

Practice noticing what's in your environment right this very minute:

I See: _____

I Feel: _____

I Hear: _____

I Smell: _____

I Taste: _____

I FEEL...

Many of us have not been taught much about feelings. I encourage clients to really notice how their body feels when experiencing an emotion. If you feel tightness in your chest, for example, you might realize you've been triggered. This type of familiarity can help guide you to consciously choose to help yourself *before* the feeling grows. Ex: You notice your heart beating fast and choose to walk away feeling merely annoyed, before that annoyance morphs into despair or rage.

Positive Emotions: Open, Calm, Centered, Content, Fulfilled, Patient, Peaceful, Present, Relaxed, Serene, Trusting, Alive, Joyful, Amazed, Awed, Delighted, Eager, Ecstatic, Enchanted, Energized, Engaged, Excited, Free, Happy, Inspired, Invigorated, Passionate, Radiant, Refreshed, Rejuvenated, Satisfied, Thrilled, Courageous, Powerful, Adventurous, Brave, Capable, Confident, Determined, Grounded, Proud, Strong, Worthy, Loving, Accepting, Affectionate, Compassionate, Present, Safe, Worthy, Curious, Fascinated, Interested, Intrigued, Involved, Stimulated, Grateful, Humbled, Lucky, Moved, Thankful, Hopeful, Encouraged, Expectant, Optimistic, Trusting

Negative Emotions: Angry, Annoyed, Agitated, Bitter, Contempt, Cynical, Disdain, Disgruntled, Disturbed, Exasperated, Frustrated, Furious, Grouchy, Impatient, Irritated, Irate, Moody, Outraged, Resentful, Upset, Depressed, Disappointed, Discouraged, Forlorn, Heartbroken, Hopeless, Lonely, Longing, Weary, Disconnected, Numb (yes, numb is a feeling), Bored, Confused, Distant, Empty, Indifferent, Isolated, Resistant, Shut Down, Uneasy, Embarrassed, Ashamed, Humiliated, Inhibited, Mortified, Self-conscious, Worthless, Afraid, Nervous, Paralyzed, Scared, Terrified, Worried, Fragile, Powerless

WAYS TO DEAL WITH UPSETTING THOUGHTS

Many people tend to worry more than is helpful. Learning to guide your thoughts can be freeing. I'm not encouraging you to totally ignore the difficult stuff in your life, .

- *Notice your thought and picture dropping it like a hot coal before it burns you.*

- *Imagine that you are stuffing your unhelpful thoughts into an empty balloon. Fill the balloon with helium and release it into the atmosphere. Watch it float up into the atmosphere, taking the unhelpful thoughts away.*

- *Imagine putting your troubling thoughts onto a shelf in your mind. You know where they are and you can decide if and when to revisit these issues.*

- *Set aside a specific time of day to worry for 10-15 minutes. Only allow yourself to think about these worries during the allotted time period.*

- *Treat your worries like the gas you may get after eating a big meal. Your body and mind are processing. Let the unpleasant thoughts pass. Let them go.*

PROGRESSIVE MUSCLE RELAXATION

Imagine that you're holding a lemon in each hand. Squeeze each one as hard as you can. Release and relax. Notice how your arms feel different.

You can use this relaxation technique for your entire body to help you fall asleep. *When you're in bed, starting with your feet, squeeze each of the different muscle groups tightly. End with your face. Squeeze and release all of the muscle groups. If you're still awake, notice the feeling of relaxation.*

4-SQUARE BREATHING

You can use 4-Square Breathing if you're ever feeling overwhelmed or anxious. You could also use this tool if and when you notice yourself having unhelpful thoughts or fears (ex: "I am a loser"). Breathing through these mental blocks can help you to experience success.

- *Breathe in through your nose for 4 seconds*
- *Hold your breath for 4 seconds*
- *Exhale through your mouth for 4 seconds*

IF YOUR BODY FEELS UNCOMFORTABLE

These exercises are for relieving occasional pain and discomfort. Please see your doctor if you are experiencing significant discomfort or need medical attention.

- *Close your eyes and focus inside yourself.*
- *Observe any feelings of discomfort or pain.*
- *Identify what these feelings are seeking to communicate.*
- *Formulate a soothing mantra that addresses this need, such as "Cool, gentle pressure."*
- *Quietly or aloud, repeat this affirmation.*

You can keep track of your soothing statements here:

WHAT IS YOUR BODY SAYING NOW?

WHAT CAN YOU CONTROL?

If you're worried, it can help to think about what's in your control and what isn't. Usually, what we can control has to do with ourselves.

Do you have things you routinely worry about? Do you wish other people would change? That's normal of course, but if you focus instead on how you'd like respond, communicate, behave, and care for yourself, you may feel a lot better.

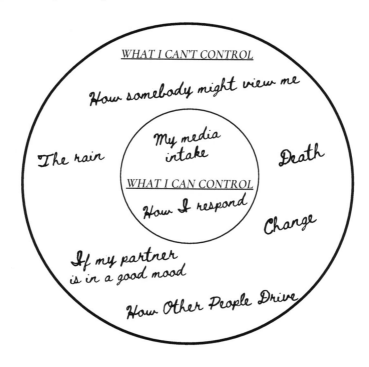

WHAT CAN YOU CONTROL?

Note the things you can control in the inner circle and the things you cannot control in the outer circle.

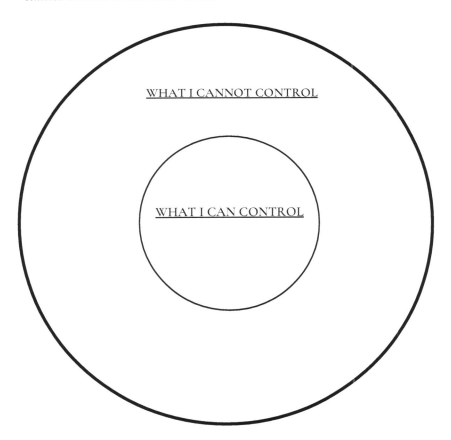

STAND UP TO YOUR INNER BULLY

Anxious thoughts can bully you. For instance, you might have a part that says, "Who do you think you are?" or "You can't do that!" or "You're going to embarrass yourself *again*."

These worrisome messages might sound like a parent or an older sibling. These parts may have developed as a way to keep you safe, but now they may be holding you back. If you're ready to make a change and move past these old blocks, try this exercise.

Talk back to your inner bully or your anxious thoughts. Example:

ANXIOUS THOUGHT	TALK BACK
Everyone will laugh at you.	Most people are busy looking at their phones, not me. Plus, that's an old story from something that happened ONCE years ago. Nothing else bad has happened when I entered a room.
You're a terrible artist.	My art is unique. Janice likes it. I'm allowed to express myself. It feels good to create. I'm communing, feeling, and listening in an awesome way (in the true sense of the word.)

TALK BACK TO YOUR WORRIES

ANXIOUS THOUGHT	TALK BACK

People are just busy sometimes

WORLD-RELATED HEAVINESS

What can we do to control our anxiety and to keep from slipping into debilitating despair when we think about world events?

- *Know that you're not alone in your feelings.*
- *Identify what you can control.*
- *Notice good people doing helpful things.*
- *Limit your news intake.*
- *Do what you can. Joining with others and working toward a common goal, can help you feel more empowered.*
- *Contribute to causes you believe in, when and if you can.*
- *Act locally to make your world a more fair, equitable, and compassionate place.*
- *Remember that it's okay to take care of yourself.*
- *Be kind to yourself.*
- *Think about the ways that you already contribute toward making the world better.*
- *Do something that feels good like spending time with your pet or in nature.*
- *Exercise in order to help regulate your nervous system and move the stress out of your body.*
- *Envision a better world. Try to focus more on loving than hating.*
- *If needed, get support from a therapist or doctor, or other trusted professional.*

ONE KIND OF MEDITATION

Since studying the Law of Attraction, I've found that meditating for about 15-20 minutes a day can be life-changing. Morning seems to be an ideal time to meditate because the brain and the body haven't completely revved up yet.

It sounds simple, but the practice of meditation can provide a peaceful, powerful, and different kind of experience. It's a chance to connect with the infinite, essential part of yourself and to quiet your mind. You can tune into the clarity of your well-being.

Set a timer for 10-15 minutes. It's fine to sit or to lie down if that's more comfortable. Either way works. Just try to be in a place where you won't be disturbed.

Focus on a sound like a recording of static or an electric fan or air conditioning. These types of sounds are not interesting, and so they usually won't lead to other thoughts that might feel negative. You could imagine merging yourself with the sound. Take a break from your mind chatter. Notice your thoughts without judgment, as if they are leaves floating by in a stream.

NOTES ON MEDITATION

Do you enjoy meditating? Have you found any guided recordings that you like? Do you have any thoughts about meditation? Write all about them.

GETTING HELP FROM YOUR SENSES

On the following pages, identify some positively-associated things that relate to your senses. These should be things that you enjoy or that you feel neutral about. They shouldn't evoke any challenging emotions like sadness or longing. Try to stay in the "Neutral to Good" Zone. You can use these elements to help soothe you.

What do you like the look of? What images calm you (ex: redwood trees, ocean, the color blue)?

What do you like the feel of (ex: dog's fur, pebbles, sand)?

GETTING HELP FROM YOUR SENSES

What do you like the smell of (ex: lemons, bread, roses)?

What do you like to listen to (ex: rain, dog lapping water, laughter, etc.)?

FILL YOUR WORLD WITH ROCKS

Add more soothing things into your daily environment. For example:

- *If you like the feel of rocks, go outside and find one that feels right to you. Carry it in your pocket. Touch it throughout the day. Or put a rock on your desk*
- *Or you can buy yourself flowers*
- *Make a collage of your sense-related resources*
- *Add photos of your objects to the screen on your phone*
- *Write a list and hang it up in your home where you'll see it, or take a photo of your list and put it on your phone*

INCORPORATE SOOTHING EXPERIENCES

How might you incorporate more soothing elements into your everyday life?

CHANGE THE CHANNEL IN YOUR MIND

When we choose our thoughts more mindfully, our feelings follow suit.

How to change the channel in your mind:

- *Notice when you're having an unhelpful thought (you'll know because you'll feel bad).*
- *Imagine you're holding a remote control. Use it to change the channel in your mind to a more pleasant channel. Think about any of the sense-related resources from the previous exercise.*
- *Keep replacing unhelpful thoughts with good-feeling thoughts.*

What are some of your favorite "thought channels" to tune to? I often think about my dog Marvin's ears flapping while he walks along.

THOUGHT-ERASING

This technique is not as dystopian as it sounds.

You can erase thoughts whenever they bother you. If you're up in the middle of the night worrying about things.

Here's how to erase unhelpful thoughts:

1. *Notice Your Annoying/Scary/Worrisome Thought*
2. *Imagine it visually. Maybe you'll see a picture of the words typed out or written, or you may picture a scene*
3. *Now see your own hand holding a chalkboard eraser*
4. *Erase the thought until it's gone*
5. *Repeat as often as necessary*

Or you can envision giant words made from pieces of wood spelling out your troubling thought. Then bring in a fire-breathing dragon to incinerate the words.

THROW OUT THE TRASH

Here's another technique for eliminating unhelpful thoughts.

1. *Notice when you're having a garbage thought about yourself (examples: "I'm an idiot." "Nobody likes me." "I'm hideous.")*
2. *Feel into your body. Where does that thought live within you? Locate it.*
3. *Now imagine you're reaching into that place and extract the garbage. Get it all.*
4. *Imagine throwing the garbage out. Or you can envision a garbage disposal or toilet near you. Throw in the unhelpful thoughts. Then turn on the disposal or flush the toilet.*
5. *Repeat if necessary.*

GARBAGE THOUGHTS TO GET RID OF

Remember to imagine getting rid of these thoughts. You don't need to carry them with you anymore.

LET YOUR BODY CHOOSE

Our bodies and emotions are amazing tools for decision-making.

Think about a decision you're trying to make. Close your eyes and imagine holding one decision in your hand. What do you feel in your body? Does the option feel light and relieving, or heavy and sticky? Does it feel cloudy or murky? Does it feel fun and exciting? Write down your impressions. Now do the same with your other options. What feels best?

OPTION A	OPTION B
HOW OPTION A FEELS	**HOW OPTION B FEELS**

IF YOU MUST INTERACT WITH SOMEBODY WHO REMINDS YOU OF A PERSON WHO UNNERVES YOU

Once in awhile, the wheels of life bring us a totally new person (or situation) who reminds us eerily of another person (or situation) that we've had trouble or trauma with. This can really throw us off our game. We know that this person is not the other one, but our emotions get mixed up just the same. As Bessel Van der Kolk says, "The Body Keeps the Score." Our bodies react to sensory cues, and so we can react as if they were the same person, despite knowing they are different people. So what can we do?

On the next page, identify things that the two different people (or situations) have in common. Then write down how they are not at all the same.

Really notice the differences. Feel the differences. Focus on the differences.

The more you note the differences, the more calm you will most likely feel.

Focus on the differences. Feel the differences.

	Current Person/Situation	Past Person/Situation
SIMILARITIES		
DIFFERENCES		

YOUR ENERGETIC SAFETY SUIT

This exercise works well if you know you'll be in a challenging environment where you anticipate feeling vulnerable.

Imagining a protective energetic suit around you helps you maintain healthy boundaries. This magical suit keeps good feelings close to you and difficult energy out.

How to Create Your Energy Suit:

Sit or lie down and focus on your spine's base and picture your energy collecting there. Envision a power line, a root, or a ray of energy shooting down from that your body into the earth, moving through dirt layers and rock.

Now, bring that earthly energy back up through the cord, up through your spine's base, then up your back, forging a super-bond with the Earth.

Move the energy up to any tense spots in your back. Just notice how you feel. Notice if there is any damage to your energy suit and if there is, see yourself mending the rips or banging out the dings.

Any potentially harmful energy should stay outside of your energetic safety suit. Envision unwanted energy bouncing off the suit's surface, keeping you feeling good and safe inside.

ENERGETIC BOUNDARIES ARE HELPFUL

Think of situations where an energetic boundary could help.

What does your energetic suit look like?

Does your safe energy suit fit over your whole body, like a space suit or full-body footsie, zip-up pajamas that also go over your head? You might want to make sure that your suit is totally zipped up. Or, you can protect yourself by imagining a protective radiant light surrounding your body. The light should be a healing color. What's a healing color for you?

COMMUNICATING WITHOUT FEAR

I used to feel really frightened whenever I had to make phone calls (which was awfully often before texting). Calling people I don't know is still not my favorite thing, but I've found that the following tips have helped me to feel calmer and more confident while dialing:

1. *Pretend you're talking to a friend (unless that's hard).*
2. *Before calling, make a list of things you want to say.*
3. *If it's up your alley, you could practice saying aloud what you want to say before you call.*
4. *Imagine that the other person is kind and understanding.*
5. *If you need a subject to fill the air space, talk about the weather or ask how the other person's day is going.*
6. *Realize that most people pay more attention to themselves than to you.*
7. *Tell yourself that all will go well.*

PAUSE FOR ALIGNMENT

Sometimes we feel obligated to give people answers right away, before we're sure what's best for us, Answering on the spot can lead to bad choices that don't align with our values, needs, preferences, or safety.

Instead of impulsively blurting out an answer in order to not appear stupid or to placate someone, you could say, "I'm not sure. I'll get back to you." Taking time to do research or to process feelings about a decision is a smart and responsible thing to do.

Giving yourself time may feel strange or nerve-wracking at first. It can feel scary to take up space, especially if you weren't allowed to do that in your family. Sometimes this behavior develops as a coping strategy to stay safe. If you currently feel unsafe or are being threatened by someone in your life, please seek assistance.

In general, I've found that the more you practice taking up space, the easier it becomes. You are worthy, and your feelings are just as important as everyone else's.

THE ART OF THE PREFACE

Are you ever nervous in social situations? I am, too. Do you worry that other people might think you're weird and reject you? Me too. This imperfect tip has helped me to feel less frightened and ashamed in public. Maybe it will help you, too.

Here's how "The Art of the Preface" works:

1. *You're worried about talking with people because you feel gross.*
2. *Someone begins to approach. What should you do?*
3. *Say "hello." Then preface anything else you're about to say with a statement like, "Hi! Before I say anything more, I just want to mention that I didn't get a lot of sleep last night and so I might mess up my words a bit." But that might be a lie, and you might want to tell the truth. So instead you could say, "Oh, hi. I was just realizing that I'm a bit out of practice having a conversation. Please forgive my rustiness. How are you?"*

I realize that this may sound like a half-baked strategy, but this technique can offer a stepping stone towards comfort. You introduce your nervousness before it hijacks you. You have taken your control back. This coping method can help you focus on connecting with the other person rather than worrying. BTW, you're not gross.

THE ART OF THE PREFACE

Can you think of a time you might use the Prefacing technique? What might you say? If you're nervous about any situation, it can provide some cushioning. In my experience, when we accept ourselves, we tend to feel more relaxed and other people feel more relaxed being around us.

A FORMULA FOR EXPRESSING FEELINGS

This is a helpful tool for expressing your feelings in a safe and respectful way.

The formula:

1. *When I heard you say (blank), or when you did (blank),*
2. *I felt (blank).*
3. *In the future, I'd like to ask that you (blank).*

This formula can work well because while using it, you are referencing a mutually agreed-upon fact. (The sauerkraut was indeed left out on the counter.) The other person is more likely to be receptive to your words because you're speaking about your own feelings. ("When I saw the jar of artisanal sauerkraut on the counter and you were not home, I felt frustrated.") Feelings aren't wrong or right. They just are. Then you could state a request. ("Next time, could you please put the sauerkraut back in the fridge before you leave?") Your roommate may or may not put the sauerkraut away next time, but at least you'll know you have expressed yourself in a kind and constructive way. And you have let the other person know how their behavior has affected you.

EXPRESS YOURSELF

Think about some situations where the following communicative formula might come in handy: When I heard you say (blank), or when you did (blank), I felt (blank). In the future, I'd like to ask that you (blank). Practice here.

VALIDATION SANDWICH

You can use the Validation Sandwich technique anytime that you need to communicate something, and you're pretty certain that the other person doesn't want to hear it.

Picture a sandwich with two slices of bread surrounding your filling of choice. This technique is simple. The "bread" of compassion softens the blow. The bread is nice stuff. The filling is the difficult communication. After you "deliver" the filling, you add a kind comment. This method can help you know that you've done your best. Ideally, the other person will feel acknowledged, rather than simply criticized.

1. First, say something that you appreciate about the person or situation (bread)

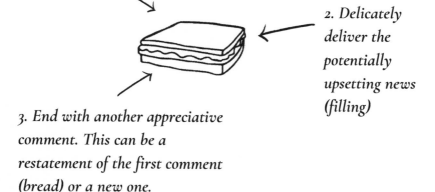

2. Delicately deliver the potentially upsetting news (filling)

3. End with another appreciative comment. This can be a restatement of the first comment (bread) or a new one.

VALIDATION SANDWICH

Can you think of an instance when you might use the Validation Sandwich approach? What's the bread? What's the filling? Ex: "I think it's cool how you've almost reached the bonus stage in your game (bread). But to be honest, I hate seeing and smelling your dirty dishes in the sink. I just wanted to let you know that I'm not going to wash them for you anymore so you're going to need to start doing it (filling). Good luck with your game (bread)."

PRACTICE SAYING NO WITH A FRIEND

Do you have a hard time saying no? Do you worry that others will become upset or reject you if you assert yourself? Do you often comply out of habit, even when the outcomes are less-than-stellar?

If you answered yes to any of the above questions, you might benefit from the following exercise. I've titled it "Practice Saying No with a Friend," but if you'd like to do this one alone, that is 100% fine. We have the technology.

1. Make a list of things you're sure that you don't like. (Riding in the middle seat, descending into vertical caves, the smell of the fish counter, the itch that comes after 3 days of not shaving your legs, etc.)
2. Have your friend (or yourself) ask you questions like, "Do you want to go on a 5-hour flight sitting in the middle seat with two sleeping people on either side of you?" or "Do you want to prepare this 10-pound salmon?" Each statement should elicit the desire to say no.
3. Answer "No!" to each of the questions using as much enthusiasm as you want to. The repetition of and engagement with the word "no" in this exercise can feel freeing, freeing, freeing. Practicing boundaries in a safe and friendly forum helps us to build resilience and lets our bodies understand that saying no is an okay thing to do.

THE REJECTION CONNECTION

Most people have felt rejected at some point in life. Rejection hurts. There are some things we can do to ease the pain of rejection.

1. *Acknowledge to yourself that you are hurting.*
2. *Be kind to yourself. Often you haven't personally done or said anything to be rejected. Sometimes people just forget to include us, or circumstances come into play like room capacity, or cost. Or maybe the rejecter isn't ready to be with a scintillating, healthy partner like yourself.*
3. *Identify your own valuable traits--as a potential partner, friend, captivating social companion, diligent student, or dependable team member.*
4. *Ask yourself if there's anything you can learn from this experience.*
5. *Think about whether you may have dodged a bad situation by being rejected. Sometimes we aren't actually a good fit with something or someone, even when we really wish we were.*
6. *Do something creative or dig in the garden.*
7. *Do something social so that you feel more connected.*
8. *Talk to yourself like you would a friend.*
9. *Think of all the people all over the globe who feel the same way as you do at the same moment. You're not alone.*

THE REJECTION CONNECTION

If you're ever feeling rejected, list your valuable traits. (Ex: If you were not invited to a party, you could write "I'm hilarious and thoughtful"):

What might you say to a friend if they were in the same position?

HOW TO FEEL GOOD BEING YOURSELF

We humans tend to worry about what other people think of us. Sometimes it feels like we're putting ourselves out there just to be judged. So what can we do?

1. *Know that there's nothing wrong with you for having worries related to fitting in. Wanting to belong is a primal desire.*
2. *Understand that you're a valuable and unique person, just as every other person is unique. Some people will resonate with you and others won't. It's like chemistry. We don't and cannot bond with everyone, even if we feel like we're meant to do so.*
3. *Become aware of and align with your own values. When we slow down enough to act from our values, we feel more in tune with ourselves.*
4. *Remember that we can't control how other people react to us. Realize that their reactions often have zero to do with us. People get cranky, busy, overwhelmed, and distracted. If someone is grouchy with us, that really doesn't mean that they don't like us. Everyone has their own baggage. Some people feel compelled to be mean or critical. It's not about you.*
5. *If you're feeling vulnerable, surround yourself with people you trust. If you can't find those people, then go to a coffee shop or library. You might want to contact a nice therapist.*
6. *Know that you are allowed to take up space. Be your own best friend. Congratulate yourself for allowing yourself to shine.*

INNER RESOURCES & EMDR THERAPY

One way that we EMDR therapists prepare clients to process traumatic experiences is to make sure that the client first identifies inner supports. These internal resources come from the client's own experience and can help the client to feel safer while processing trauma. These resources can also provide corrective emotional experiences. On the following pages, you'll identify some of your own inner resources that you can draw upon whenever you need support.

Very, very simply explained, EMDR (Eye Movement Desensitization and Reprocessing) is an evidence-based psychotherapy trauma treatment modality discovered and developed by the psychologist Francine Shapiro. EMDR utilizes the client's emotions, body sensations, beliefs about self, a guided stream of consciousness, imagination, and bilateral stimulation to facilitate healing from trauma. EMDR tends to the body, mind, and spirit. In EMDR therapy, the client moves naturally toward healing, guided by the therapist.

Please visit EMDR.com to read more about this transformative type of therapy.

TRANQUIL PLACE

Write about a place that feels good to you, peaceful and relaxing. It can be someplace you've been in real life or a place you've only seen in a movie or read about in a book. It can be totally made up or it could be your couch at home.

Imagine as many details as possible. What are the smells and sounds? What is the temperature like? What do you see?

If it's hard for you to imagine a Tranquil place, you can substitute your favorite color or tree.

My Tranquil Place is:

TRANQUIL PLACE

What positive feelings do you notice in your body when you think of being in this place?

_____

_____

_____

_____

What emotions do you feel?

_____

_____

_____

_____

Are any other thoughts coming to your mind when you think about this Tranquil Place? If so, jot them down here.

_____

_____

CARING INDIVIDUAL

Identify a Caring Individual. This figure can be a person from your everyday life (like a good friend), or it could be a fictional character or famous person. This figure could be a loving pet or grandparent. We're looking for someone or something that represents the qualities of caring.

If it's hard to imagine someone nurturing you, can you see an animal taking care of its young? I like to picture a mother gorilla looking into the eyes of her baby. Your Caring Individual could even be a special blanket or sweatshirt.

As you imagine this Caring Individual, what do you notice in your body? What emotions do you feel?

Caring Individual(s):

CARING INDIVIDUAL

What good feelings do you notice in your body when you think of being in the presence of this figure?

What emotions do you feel?

Are any other thoughts coming to your mind when you think about this Caring Individual? If so, note them now.

THE DEFENDER

Can you envision a Defender? This can be a real person from your life or a fictional character or a famous person. This individual should be someone you can imagine "has your back."

Some people imagine a superhero, guardian angel, or video game character. Or your defender figure could be an animal, such as a lion, wildcat, or wolf.

If it's hard to imagine someone protecting you, maybe you can picture an animal protecting its young? Like a bear with cubs, for example?

If this one is hard, it's okay to think about a force field, protective energetic suit, or a shield.

Defender(s):

THE DEFENDER

What positive feelings do you notice in your body when you think of being in the presence of this individual? If you identify more than one, write about both here.

What emotions do you feel?

Are any other thoughts coming to your mind when you think about the Defender? If so, what are they?

INSIGHTFUL INDIVIDUAL

Think of an Insightful Individual. This person can be from your everyday life, or they can be a fictional character like Yoda or Dumbledore. Or maybe you connect to a historical figure or YouTube personality that you admire. Your Insightful Individual could be an animal or a tree.

If it's hard to imagine someone giving you guidance, can you picture a scene from a movie where a kind teacher is helping a student understand something? We're looking for the feeling that goes along with being guided by a trustworthy figure.

Picture this individual being actively wise. Notice what you feel in your body. What positive emotions do you feel?

Insightful Individual(s):

INSIGHTFUL INDIVIDUAL

What positive feelings do you notice in your body when you think of being in the presence of this individual?

What emotions do you feel?

Are any other thoughts coming to your mind when you think about the Insightful Individual? If so, describe your thoughts here.

TRANSCENDENT INDIVIDUAL

Can you identify a Transcendent Individual? This person could someone you know from your life, your religion, or they could be from a a sacred text, from history, or even from a movie. It could be an angel, or a book, a tree, lavender light, or crystal. It's up to you. This exercise is about your own unique connection.

We're looking for the feeling that goes along with being guided. Picture this figure or element emitting transcendent, spiritual guidance. Notice what you feel in your body. What positive emotions do you feel?

Transcendent Individual(s):

TRANSCENDENT INDIVIDUAL

What positive feelings do you notice in your body when you think of being in their presence?

What pleasant emotions do you feel?

Are any other thoughts coming to your mind when you think about the Transcendent Individual? If so, describe your thoughts here.

WONDER TEAM POWERS ACTIVATE

Imagine all of your resource figures in a circle around you, maybe gathered together in your Tranquil Place. Look around the circle at them. Take in the feelings of support. You deserve to feel good.

You can call upon your inner dream team whenever needed or desired. Every time you do this, you're strengthening your positive neural connections. You're helping yourself build resilience because you're experiencing the feelings of being supported, cared for, protected, and guided. So even if you never got this kind of support as a child, you can provide it to yourself now. (I have been taught that on some level, our brains don't know the difference between real, lived experiences and imagined ones. That's why peak performance visualization work so well. So why not imagine a magical support team?)

MY TEAM

Caring Individual(s):

Defender Individual(s):

Insightful Individual(s):

Transcendent Individual(s):

I AM SUPPORTED

What is it like to feel that you have a team of allies? How does it feel to have support you can call upon? Are there any feelings coming up that want attention?

A LOVE LETTER TO YOURSELF

Here's yet another chance to be nice to yourself. (Luckily, chances will keep coming every single day.) This one may feel weird but like many therapy exercises, it can be quite powerful.

Write a love letter to yourself filled with words of kindness and understanding. If you don't feel like you can do that, could you imagine writing a letter to a friend who's in a similar situation as you?

What words would feel good and would help you or the friend feel truly understood and comforted? Ex: "I see you. I hear you. I love you. You don't have to do anything for me to love you."

A LOVE LETTER TO YOURSELF

You are a
good person

APPRECIATION & GRATITUDE

It's no secret that practicing gratitude can help us to feel happier. What we focus on tends to grow. Observing the way the universe works on your behalf can become a habit that makes you feel good. Chances are that the more often you do it, the more confident and secure you will feel. Happier, too. Uplift yourself by noticing what is going well.

Whenever we engage in the act of appreciation, we're in essence asking the universe for what we want, not for what we don't want.

I APPRECIATE

I'M GRATEFUL FOR

I APPRECIATE

BYPASS INTENSE ANXIOUS SPIRALING

The act of noticing our thoughts lights up a different part of the brain and makes self-soothing more accessible. Whatever emotion is arising, you can shift to a more functional place when you notice it.

Noticing our feelings and thoughts interrupts that spiraling pattern. Say out loud or silently something like, "I'm noticing anxiety." "I'm feeling angry." "Sadness is bubbling up." Or, "I feel self-conscious." When we practice noticing, the prefrontal cortex is activated, rather than the more reptilian reactionary area. The prefrontal cortex helps us regulate our emotions.

When we feel triggered by something in the environment, we can feel emotionally unbalanced really quickly. It can help to become familiar with our triggers so that we can recognize what's happening, and why we might be feeling so overwhelmed.

MY TRIGGERS

We may not always understand why we have the triggers we have or how they got there in the first place. Even if this is the case, it can be helpful to recognize that there are certain stimuli that activate our fight/flight/freeze/fawn responses.

List any of your triggers here:

THE ISSUES IN THE TISSUES

Most people have something they're working on, something they wish they'd do better, and hurts they wish they didn't feel. Sometimes we feel alone, like we're the only one dealing with a particular issue. This is almost never the case.

On the following pages, you'll write briefly about some issues or thoughts that are bothering you. In this book, we're primarily focused on strengthening positive neural networks rather than exploring problems deeply.

However, it can be instructive to look at our harder issues. In therapy, we notice and acknowledge the presenting problems. We get history about the issues so that we can better understand what's going on, what led to the challenges, how the client feels about them, what the client believes about the issues and about the self in relation to them, etc. When we identify what isn't working, we can try something else while moving towards healing.

As you write about the issues on the next pages, see if you notice any accompanying emotions and body sensations arising. These notes can offer important information. If you plan to go to therapy, I'd encourage that you bring your notes with you. This focused attention can be really helpful.

FIRST ISSUE

What would the book or movie title of this problem be?

What emotions do you feel now when you think about this issue?

What body sensations do you feel when you think about it? Tara Brach says, "Our issues are in our tissues." Our thoughts, feelings, and actions are connected.

How old does this issue feel? When do you think it may have started?

FIRST ISSUE

Do you have any negative self-beliefs or thoughts associated with this issue? Examples: "I'm helpless," "I'm incapable," "I'm not smart enough," etc.

Imagine the type of resource you'd need to feel or respond differently? What inner strength would help you to not feel so overwhelmed, helpless, or inadequate?

Do you know anyone, whether from your personal life or from the wider world, who exemplifies this kind of strength? This person could be real or fictional, someone you know personally or just know of.

FIRST ISSUE

Imagine that you now possess this support within your own mind and body. What might that experience be like?

Envision yourself confronting the stressful situation you identified earlier, but now equipped with this strength within every part of your being.

Next, conjure a symbol, image, word, or mantra that could serve as a reminder of this strength and add it to your environment.

SECOND ISSUE

What would the book or movie title of this problem be?

What emotions do you feel now when you think about this issue?

What do you notice in your body when you think about it?

How old does this issue feel? When do you think it may have started?

SECOND ISSUE

Do you have any negative self-beliefs or thoughts associated with this issue? Examples: "I'm helpless," "I'm incapable," "I'm not smart enough," etc.

Imagine the type of resource you'd need to feel or respond differently? What inner strength would help you to not feel so overwhelmed, helpless, or inadequate?

Do you know anyone, whether from your personal life or from the wider world, who exemplifies this kind of strength? This person could be real or fictional, someone you know personally or just know of.

SECOND ISSUE
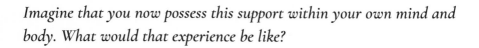

Imagine that you now possess this support within your own mind and body. What would that experience be like?

Envision yourself confronting the stressful situation you identified earlier, but now equipped with this strength within every part of your being.

Next, conjure a symbol, image, word, or mantra that could serve as a reminder of this strength and add it to your environment.

THIRD ISSUE

What would the book or movie title of this problem be?

What emotions do you feel now when you think about this issue?

What body sensations do you feel when you think about it?

How old does this issue feel? When do you think it may have started?

THIRD ISSUE

Do you have any negative self-beliefs or thoughts associated with this issue? Examples: "I'm helpless," "I'm incapable," "I'm not smart enough," etc.

Imagine the type of resource you'd need to feel or respond differently? What inner strength or assistance would help you to not feel so overwhelmed, helpless, or inadequate?

Do you know anyone, whether from your personal life or from the wider world, who exemplifies this kind of strength? This person could be real or fictional, someone you know personally or just know of.

THIRD ISSUE

Imagine that you now possess this support within your own mind and body. What would that experience be like?

Envision yourself confronting the stressful situation you identified earlier, but now equipped with this strength within every part of your being.

Next, conjure a symbol, image, word, or mantra that could serve as a reminder of this strength and add it to your environment.

YOU ARE RESILIENT

Keep track of times when you thought you couldn't do something, but somehow you did it anyway.

What happened? How did you cope? What helped?

I did that somehow

EARLY DAYDREAMS

When you were a kid, who or how did you want to be when grew up? How and where did you want to live? Did you daydream regularly? If so, how did daydreaming help you?

CARLY DAYDRCAMS

Did you tell anyone about these dreams of yours, or did you keep them to yourself? Why or why not? If you shared your dreams (whether nighttime or daytime) how did the listener respond? And has this had an effect on you?

WHERE DO YOU WANT TO GO?

What are some of your goals? What would you like to change or transform in your life?

WHERE DO YOU WANT TO GO?

How would you know that you were moving closer to the changes that you want to experience?

ILLUMINATING YOUR FOUNDATION

Let's point our flashlights into the caverns of your history, which may or may not include difficult things that have happened to you. You don't need to venture too deeply into the details. If this exercise is causing you any anxiety, feel free to take a breather or just skip it. It's okay to back out of the cave.

Sometimes people don't remember their histories very well, and they can worry about this. Not remembering can happen for a variety of reasons, including if you happened to have spent a lot of time alone. We tend to remember events better if someone else was there. Maybe you blocked something out. That's not a bad thing. Our miraculous brains find ways to protect us.

Recalling how we were as children can help us to make sense of our present, allow us to reconnect with younger versions of ourselves, remind us of desires we once had, and look at the things we once liked. We may feel the same inside, or we may have grown away from the young person we once were. If there are childhood wounds that still hurt, you may want to work with a therapist to heal them.

Every child deserves love, safety, respect, shelter, and care. If you didn't receive what you needed, it's not too late. You can have reparative experiences.

ILLUMINATING YOUR FOUNDATION

Have you heard any stories related to your conception or your birth? What were you told if anything? What do you imagine if you haven't heard?

YOUR ESSENTIAL NEEDS

Do you feel in the core of your being that you got what you needed as an infant and toddler? if not, what was missing? What did you need?

EARLIEST MEMORY

What is your earliest memory? Do you feel like that memory holds a theme that has emerged throughout your life? (For example, my first memory is attempting to do a somersault with a cast on my broken arm. I tried again and again, but despite my best efforts, my execution wasn't smooth. I kept rolling off to the side instead of fluidly forward. This feeling of frustration feels familiar and has shown up in various pursuits over the years like with my art.)

A GOOD DISPOSITION

What were you like as a baby or very little child? Did they say you had a "good disposition" or not so much? When you look back at videos or photos of yourself, what emotions do you feel? Can you extend warmth to this little version of yourself, or is it hard to?

BLUEBERRIES FOR BERNARD

What were some of your favorite foods when you were little? If you don't remember, what have you heard?

When you think of yourself as a baby or toddler, what do you remember liking or finding comfort in? Did you have a favorite stuffed animal or blanket?

IMAGINARY FRIENDS?

What activities did you like to do when you were in preschool or
kindergarten? Did you have an imaginary friend? How did you
feel with that imaginary friend? Did anyone know? If so, how did
they respond to the existence of this friend?

The author's friend

THE ELEMENTARY YEARS

What were you like as an elementary school-age child? When you look at videos or photos of yourself, what emotions do you feel? If you have a photo now, you could try putting it in front of you. Feel what you feel. (You could keep a photo of yourself in this book.)

THE ELEMENTARY YEARS

Was anything very difficult for you or your family when you were an elementary school-age child? What might you have needed that you didn't get?

FERDINAND & FRENCH FRIES

What were some favorite toys or books in elementary school?

What were some of your favorite foods or food-related experiences in elementary school?

SHIMMYING UP ROPES

What activities did you like to do in elementary school?

What did you like about yourself when you were elementary school-age? (Even if no one knew this about you.)

MRS. THADY AND ME

Who were your favorite teachers, coaches, group leaders, or other adults when you were young? Did any of them see you, or say something that stuck with you?

She liked my essay about polar bears

EARLY CONNECTIONS

Who were your favorite friends? If you lacked friends, who were you drawn to? Which peers did you admire? Who sticks out in your memory for whatever reason?

What did you like to do outside of school during the elementary years? Include any favorite activities or memories.

THE TEEN YEARS

During the high school years, did you feel supported and valued by your family or community? What support did you need during that time?

TEEN TACTICS

What were you like as a teenager? How did you cope?

Dunno

MY TEENAGE WORLD

What were some of your favorite possessions, music, shows, song lyrics, movies, video games, or books when you were a teenager?

What were your favorite foods when you were a teen?

IN MY SPHERE

What activities did you like to do when you were high school age?

Who were important teachers, coaches, group leaders, or bosses or other adults during the high school-age years? (Positive influences)

INFLUENCES

Did you have favorite friends or peers when you were a teenager?

Did you have any role models when you were a teenager? Who did you want to be like?

INFLUENCES

How was your teenage bedroom decorated?

What was your favorite hangout during these years?

ACTIVITIES

What did you like to do outside of school during those years? Any jobs or sports?

Any favorite family activities, vacations, or memories during the teen years?

THE EARLY ADULT YEARS

After the high school years, if you went to college or not, did you feel supported and valued by your family or community? What support did you require during that time? Did you get it?

I AM OKAY AND MAYBE EVEN SPECIAL

What positive words would you use to describe yourself?

Okay
Special

RESONANCE IN THE OUTER WORLD

What were/are some of your favorite music, shows, song lyrics, video games, or books when you were a young adult?

FUN IS GOOD

What activities were (or are) fun?

Are there activities you think would be fun but haven't tried yet?

POSITIVE AFFIRMATIONS

Reciting positive affirmations can disrupt negative thought patterns, cheer you on, and help you to power through challenging moments. Here are a few that have helped me: "Everything is okay. I'm doing the best I can. I've got good intentions. I'm allowed to change and grow. In fact, it's awesome to change and grow. I'm right where I need to be."

Positive Affirmations

POWER, JOY, FLOW & CONNECTION

Can you remember a time when you felt actively powerful and in control?

Maybe it's when you were kind to someone, or were playing sports, or doing a household task like washing the dishes (better than anyone ever has).

Notice the details. Tune into your emotions and body feelings. Focus on the positive elements, write about them.

A MOMENT OF JOY

Do you remember a moment when you felt joy or elation? Notice your body feelings and the details. Write about this moment, and then write an "I am" sentence that encapsulates the positive feeling you had about yourself while doing this activity.

I am

A STATE OF FLOW

Do you remember a time when things seemed to flow for you? Maybe you were creating art or singing a song. This can be a small moment. Tune into your emotions and body feelings. Focus on the positive elements, write about them, and then write an "I am" sentence that encapsulates the positive feeling you had about yourself while you experienced this feeling of Flow.

I am

CONNECTION TO THE UNIVERSE

Can you remember a time when you felt positively connected to the universe, to the greater world, to your spirituality, to your life purpose, or to your ancestors? As you write, tune into your emotions and body feelings. Are any positive messages coming through to you?

I am

PROMPTS TO LIGHT YOUR WAY

You can activate your inner guidance system by focusing on what has felt good and deeply meaningful. You can remember who you really are, who you have always been, apart from the potentially cruddy things that may have happened to you. This is a chance to connect with yourself in a new way.

The following prompts were designed to elicit positive thoughts and feelings that already exist inside of you. Basking in these warm feelings can help strengthen your positively-oriented neural pathways. When we know and can identify what feels right for us, we can make more aligned choices more of the time. We can base our future choices on what we recognize has helped us to feel safe, interested, excited, soothed, and principled in the past.

Making decisions becomes much easier, and that's something to celebrate.

I AM SUCCESSFUL

How are some ways you are already successful? Even small examples count.

What's the most helpful advice you've received?

I HAVE A BIT OF WISDOM

What advice would you give to your younger self or to another young person?

I AM KIND

Tell about a time you were kind when you didn't need to be.

I OFTEN KNOW WHAT'S WHAT

Sometimes, we're confused. Feelings of confusion can make us feel lost in all areas, but we can focus on something else that we are you clear about. This helps to alleviate distress. What do you know? If you're not sure what you know, can you identify what you don't want? If you do this, it's much easier to figure out what you'd prefer. Here's an example: "I am not sure if I want to go out for pizza with people, or if I'd prefer to stay home and eat salad alone. There are so many variables. I know that I love pizza and I like salad. I know that I enjoy this group except that I feel nervous around one of them. I know that I usually am fine at home but often feel lonely and bored. I know that I'd like to go out and find a way to deal with my nervousness. Pizza is delicious."

I AM A CREATOR

When do you feel the most creative? Write about your creativity.

I AM A NATURAL

Reflect on a time you felt connected to nature.

Do you have a favorite hike, campsite, beach or other place that you like to visit? How do you feel there?

I AM A TRAVELER

Where has been your favorite place to travel? What about that place was good for you?

I'M IN THE CENTER OF IT ALL

Identify some things you like about your home or neighborhood or town.

ROFL LOL

Remember a time that you laughed more than usual.

BEING THIRSTY IS NORMAL

What do you think about when you think about drinking water? What is your preferred way to get hydrated?

Are you thirsty in other ways? (It's normal for human beings to desire connection, attention, and recognition.)

I FEEL DRAMATIC RESONANCE

What are your favorite tv shows, movies, or plays? Have any moved you deeply?

I RECOGNIZE ANCESTRAL WISDOM

What helpful messages have been handed down, either aloud or silently?

I VIBRATE LOVE AND SEND A SIGNAL

What qualities do you find attractive in an ideal mate?

I AM VALUABLE

What would you like to be seen as or recognized for?

I OBSERVE, FEEL & ABSORB

Do you have any favorite artists and/or artworks? How do they make you feel?

TUNING IN

Do you resonate with the sound of a particular musical instrument? How do feel when listening? What does it remind you of?

45s

What songs did you like to listen to (or sing) when you were a kid? What do you remember feeling back then? If you listen to (or sing) one of these songs now, how do you feel? What was your first album or strong feeling about a song?

I HAVE SWAY

What are some of your favorite ways to move your body?

I AM LIMITLESS

What are some things you'd like to try doing, if limitations weren't an issue?

I VISUALIZE A CLEAR PATH

Do you want to achieve something but feel that doubt, fear, or circumstances are getting in your way? If so, you could try this exercise:

1. *Sit in comfortable clothes in a place where you won't be disturbed. (Do not try this while driving.)*
2. *Breathe in a circular way. In through your mouth, hold it, then out through your mouth. Do this a few times. Focus on your breath. If you get dizzy, stop.*
3. *See any blocks along the way to your goal dissolving.*
4. *See a clear, easy path to your goal.*

I FEEL DEEPLY

What are you passionate about on a soul level?

I CONTRIBUTE

What do you like most about your current job or routine (even if you hate it)? What's one word you'd use to describe the best thing that this position brings out in you?

I AM WILD

What animal or animals do you most relate to? Why?

I AM DRESSED

What clothes would you like to wear if you didn't feel self-conscious or that the clothes were too expensive?

How do you think wearing this would make you feel?

I'M COMFORTABLE

In what situations or with whom do you feel most comfortable?

I AM HERE FOR A REASON

What do you feel your life purpose is? Have you had inklings?

I HAVE GOOD TIMING

What is your ideal pace for life? When have you experienced living at that pace? Do you long for the Days of Macrame or some other time?

MY SOUL SINGS

What are some poems, quotes, or song lyrics that resonate with you today?

I AM VIBRANT

What's your favorite color? How does it make you feel? Has this color always been your favorite? Does this color have a personality?

What's your favorite number? How does it make you feel? Does this number have a personality?

I'M THE DRIVER OF MY EXPERIENCE

What kind of vehicle represents you?

Electric Broom

145

I LEARN AND GROW

Have any of your beliefs changed over the years? What led up to the change?

I LOVE LIFE

What are the some of the most beautiful things you've seen?

BASIC DREAM INTERPRETATION

- *Write down your dream (or dream fragment). Even the smallest memory can provide valuable information from your unconscious*
- *Relax and open up your senses so you can feel and remember imagery and sensations from the dream*
- *Identify any image that stands out as the most significant part of the dream*
- *Notice accompanying emotions and bodily sensations that feel linked to this image*
- *Explore what the image or images make you think of*
- *If you have a nightmare, you can rewrite the dream with an alternate ending so you can be the hero*

I can be the hero

A DREAM

Date:

What image stands out as the most significant part of the dream?

Do you notice any accompanying emotions and bodily sensations that feel linked to this image?

What does the image make you think of?

A DREAM

What image stands out as the most significant part of the dream?

Do you notice any accompanying emotions and bodily sensations that feel linked to this image?

What does the image make you think of?

A DREAM   Date:

What image stands out as the most significant part of the dream?

Do you notice any accompanying emotions and bodily sensations that feel linked to this image?

What does the image make you think of?

AN IDEAL FUTURE

Write about an ideal future. What would you like to manifest? Allow yourself to write about this in a positive way, without including real world limitations. Keep the image as positive as possible. Add as many details as you can think of. (I believe in this technique because I found an essay I written in the 3rd grade a few years ago at my mother's house. The essay was titled "Where I Want to Live in the Future," and it was spot on, describing my cohousing community down to the solar panels, fruit trees, community building, and exact number of households, 26. In the essay, we lived in a big bubble in outer space, but aside from that everything was remarkably accurate.)

Love

Music

JUMP OVER THE METAPHORICAL CANYON

Many years ago, I listened to a podcast where a famous actor was being interviewed.

The actor said that there will always be a million anxiety-provoking things that could keep him from acting. He talked about his various fears, including worries related to criticism.

"The way I move forward is that I picture all of these fears stacked up like boxcars in a canyon. Then I see myself jumping over them and landing on the other side of the canyon. Sometimes I picture that I'm riding a motorcycle. Other times, I see myself taking a huge cartoon-like jump to get across."

I've carried this inspirational story with me, and it has encouraged me when I've felt stuck with my own self-limiting beliefs and worries.

I hope that like this famous actor, you too can acknowledge your fearful thoughts without letting them stop you. You deserve to live a meaningful, happy, and dreamy life.

I AM A WORK IN PROGRESS

Are there any issues you'd like to process later in therapy?

BE KIND TO YOURSELF

A lot of people don't like to ask for help, and they've got valid reasons. That said, every single person needs help from time to time. I know that it can be tough to consider talking with a therapist. I've been there, but I'll tell you a secret. Now that I am a therapist myself, I've learned that many, many therapists are sensitive and often awkward people who have experienced difficulty themselves, and they just want to be of service.

If you are interested in finding a therapist, I encourage you to look at therapists' photos and read their bios. Connect with their energy, and let your feelings guide you. You may be able to find one in your area through psychologytoday.com.

Thank you so much for going on this journey with me. I hope that you will remember to be kind to yourself. I also hope that this book will remind you of your shining and valuable inner radiance for many years to come.

Warmly,
Ruth Fankushen aka Ru Fanku
aka "The Mini Therapist"
ruthfankushentherapy.com
www.rufanku.com
rufankushop.etsy.com

Me & You

ACKNOWLEDGMENTS

Thank you to my therapy teachers at CIIS (California Institute of Integral Studies) and also to Sara Dietzel, Laurel Parnell, Alison Teal, Constance Kaplan, Francine Shapiro, Mark Grant, Robin Shapiro, Janina Fisher, Peter Levine, Arielle Schwartz, Bessel Van der Kolk, Kristin Neff, Tara Brach, and Jim Knipe and for sharing wisdom and passion, and for helping me learn how to be a better therapist. Thank you to Esther and Abraham Hicks for getting me excited about using our feelings as inner guides. Thank you to Stephen Mitchell and his "Tao Te Ching" for guiding me through dark days.

I'm grateful to my art teachers throughout the years, to my fellow poets and artists, and to my English teachers at UC Davis including Gary Snyder and David Robertson for seeing me and for showing me how to appreciate the wilderness inside and outside of ourselves.

I am thankful for my funny, fun, and brilliant friends, including the caring therapists in my consult groups. Thank you for listening to me, supporting me, and helping me with this book. My sons Gabe and Joe magically turned me into a mother and have shown me so many kinds of beauty. My husband Roger Kunkel has helped stabilize me with his calming presence, kindness, and warmth. His omnipresent guitar playing and sense of humor have infused my life with joy. My fantastic family supports me everyday, and my cohousing neighbors fill my life with effervescence. My pets Marvin and Mini provide me with love, presence, and predictability. All of these beings have helped me more than I can express. I used to feel quite lonely, but I don't anymore.

I am also deeply and tremendously grateful to my therapy clients who have trusted me, inspired me, taught me, and who have given my life purpose.

And thank YOU for being here with me now. -Ruth Fankushen

If you enjoyed this book,
I'd be ever so thankful if you
could write a few words in a
review, wherever you
purchased this book.

THANK YOU!

Instagram.com/rufanku
rufankushop.etsy.com

NOTES

NOTES

NOTES

NOTES

NOTES

NOTES

NOTES

Made in the USA
Columbia, SC
17 June 2024

36819931R00105